POPULAR
MUSIC

The Colorado Prize
for Poetry

POPULAR
MUSIC

Stephen Burt

Center for Literary Publishing
& University Press of Colorado

Fort Collins

Set in Sabon and Futura Light.
Printed in the United States of America.

Cover illustration by Jessica L. Bennett.
Cover designed by Matt Williamson.

Library of Congress
Cataloging-in-Publication Data
Burt, Stephen L., 1971–
Popular music / Stephen Burt.
p.   cm.
ISBN 0-87081-555-5 (pbk.: alk.paper)
I. Title
1999   99-043627

2 3 4 5   04

ACKNOWLEDGMENTS

My thanks to the magazines and anthologies that have printed some of these poems in America, Britain, and Ireland, sometimes in earlier versions: *AGNI, Boston Review, Colorado Review, Columbia, Fence, Grolier Poetry Prize Annual, The Harvard Advocate, The May Anthology of Oxford and Cambridge Poetry, Metre, Oxford Poetry, Poetry Review, Tabla, Thumbscrew, Western Humanities Review*, and especially *PN Review*. Six of these poems appear in *New Poetries 2* (Manchester: Carcanet, 1999). "Altar to the Egyptian Goddess Bast" appeared in the multi-media exhibit *Come Shining*, organized by C. D. Wright and Deborah Luster.

I am grateful for assistance—emotional, practical, and intellectual—from Mary Jo Bang, Jessica Bennett, Lucie Brock-Broido, Jordan Ellenberg, Forrest Gander, Maia Gemmill, Nick Halpern, Langdon Hammer, John Hollander, Tim Kendall, Nicole Krauss, Jenn Lewin, Sara Marcus, Steve Monte, Andrew Osborn, Rob Pollard, John Redmond, Amanda Schaffer, Mike Scharf, Michael Schmidt, Adam Schwartzman, Miranda Spieler, Rachel Trousdale, Helen Vendler, Emily Walker, C. D. Wright, Jane Yeh, and Monica Youn. And to my loving and attentive parents, Jeffrey and Sandra Burt.

Poems from or after Federico Garcia Lorca and Jaime Gil de Biedma are imitations or free adaptations and should not be taken as accurate translations of their Spanish originals.

CONTENTS

3

4

for my parents

Persephone (Unplugged)

I wake in the dark. My face is a stunned
Cathode-ray tube, a pomegranate
Unharmed. If I were a girl, I would be a girl.
I hate my career, I want to go home
To Avonlea. I am a tortoise shell,
A bell on an alarm clock, a Les Paul.
There are rarely men in my dreams.

The fear in your eyes is no less real
For having bounded up from *Ariel*
Than the disappointed stars on the movie channel.
If I were only a girl, I could give you a hand.

Each afternoon the off-white trumpet-flowers
I just miss touching on my way home from work
Crumple like pillowcases, like antique gloves.
It must be the dew that lifts them
Before first light: clarinet, English horn,
Querulous soprano saxophone.
They are the hills in "Sheep in Fog,"
Tight-lipped in their straight lines.

There are rarely men in my dreams.
One time I became the famous skyscraper
Whose windows littered Boston during storms,
A sparkling skirt spiraling through updrafts.

I wake in the dark. The battle of frogs and mice
Continues under my floorboards.
Somebody from Reuters is there with a big flashlight
And a microphone on her collar. Can't you leave?
Can you take me with you to Avalon?
Can you make a prediction for 1995?
If I were a girl, I could follow you, I say.
The woman from Reuters motions me to hush.
A decisive skirmish is taking place.
The bullfrogs are winning.
All the mice are wearing my pink nightgown.

1

When we are wise we spend ninety percent of our time in the house. Then we examine the connections and transitions between houses. We check to see if our lives require clarifying or strengthening. Can we substitute a better feeling or a more effective pain? Should a plan of action be moved from the end to the middle or to the beginning of the life? Are the right people in the right places? Is this house preventing something, somehow?

—Ben Marcus, *The Age of Wire & String*

Kudzu

Inglorious, militant,
it overtook our bright
new porch. My father said its stalks

rose "faster than the eye":
like the body I hated then, and hate.
We had to yank
the screen door off its frame and throw it away.

That year, in my favorite novel,
the astronauts had trouble
with a single-minded planet whose nerves were great trees;

it had watched Earth
grow up, and had stored up thoughts
the length of continents,
which, naturally, it took forever to say.

Day-Lilies at Night

Sent to bed without supper
and half-undressed, they fear

success. They are Celia
nearing the end of *As You Like It*;

each one a planetarium
about to close for good, a buckling dome
in which stars rise, bleached stains.

*(I'll put myself in poor and mean attire
and with a kind of umber smirch my face—)*

Tongue-tied at dawn, we stay up till
the constellations part; my petals curl

into a coat I shiver in, brown lace—
The sun rides at us through thin
trees, so strong

I fall for him, for Oliver. I have
been made into something unable to live on my own.

For Elizabeth Smart

The crow is *Corvidae,* the king of her guests. It's the first
warm Sunday in Washington Square. Squirrels canter and
camp on a pollam of dirt, shag pebbles, a brick in the sun,
bold grass—

no sooner can we come out to them than they will scatter.
The lean ones follow their future mates up things, selecting
like experts the twigs that can take their weight. The other
squirrels are starting to save: one props herself on two feet,
belly out, extolling her glossy nut, sad prize. Acorns can ger-
minate underground.

Tall sonorous pot vendors pace; lobster-brisk men on stoops
hawk their used libraries in stacks—all do a swift business. A
ruddy scarf rasps in a seesaw hinge. Two men hold hands for
the first time; wind gathers white daytime litter like moths,
like eager bats, from the lady next to me, who sketches the
boils on trees with an ashen disinterest.

I know what she's doing. She wants to be somebody else.

Boys

for Andrew Osborn

Like the unsubtle edges of some lives,
these spreading, unfamiliar trees touch one
another stiff, unready for the season,
their still unfolding leaves as slim as knives,

and reticent. Last winter stole our names
for unfinished things; when ice stunted every yard,
we might have called them still-to-be-delivered,
fractional promises. We might have blamed

our distance on the weather. Now, too warm
for wool, too cold to force old snow away,
the air considers whether it will storm;
each new tree's bark is pockmarked, like a boy's

unlucky skin he will outgrow. Our youth
betrays us, never comfortable; some depth
of awkwardness repels us in these roots,
these risen shallows April's mud refutes.

"The 7:57 Express to Grand Central Will Now Arrive at 7:55"

Where the Hudson comes into its own at Ardsley
Pier, the Hudson

Line's sleek tracks correct themselves on stilts:
its mugwump, sulky trees

wave dollar bills, intransigent, profuse,
like parents' additive demands:

what do you think
do you think I'm made of

Adults,
we think to drown in obligations

we once suckled and enjoyed—
replacing the sweet, complacent boredom of children

with our resentful, garlicky fatigue.
Air scours the nearer banks;

their miniature ripples
learn to quarrel, turn and multiply.

And windless shrubs,
too low to be shaken, wear their humility

lightly:
the lucky,

to whom nothing has happened,
and already flaunting their buds, their cut teeth.

Boy Learning Hebrew

Over blessings I beat on the napkins with knives; next Shabbat I would be aperture, would be explain, would be the reasons for, correcting everything.

I slept on the couch, under cords and concave slats: nothing so concentrates the mind. Our three cats had to be kept from 101st St.; indoor, they peered and skittered past our legs in quick ripples, meant to rise.
                    I think they dreamed of meat. Mine were of oars: Ys pulled into Vs, sped flows, the wall map's sharpened Manhattan sliding south of itself into standing brakes of weeds under New Jersey. Aposiopesis, apostate. I would wake over cartage noises, the sky an embarrassed pink through iterated blinds, cigar-smells, barréd clouds.

The superstitious child migrates to dirt, corners, bread shoulders, and arid homework: appanage, aptitude. Saying alien, orient, mortal, squinting at consonants, I was their reader, their blasphemer. I had already learned

to ask for another body, and get only words.

Herzliyya

The roses' bodies flaunt their thousand
Eyes, empty, supported, as if
In diapers. Their rife
Fertility grows up against them, bound,
And chafing at the knee-high garden walls.

Their ants are as eager to touch, to show affections
As the collected family dinner companions'
Animated, indoor
Ring: the mothers stand
To watch each other pour
Clear soup from sweating pitchers into bowls.

The ocean called, once, Middle-of-the-Earth
Now bangs and bangs against the middle distance—
Somebody hanging up a phone.
And the ghost of Plath,
Whom I had hated for so long,

Holds her cool scissors
Up to my ear, insisting
That I should whisper back her anger, taunt
Them with a shame-
Ful song, beginning
Now: *this isn't what I'll ever want.*

Glass

Having been measurement
and medium, and never the thing meant;

having been hotheaded in youth
but easily coaxed, or tickled, till short of breath;

able to weep undetectably for years
and be thought solid; having been stained *his* and *hers*

through an acid process; having been chilled and sealed
with maplewood varnish and Naptha

or silvered and then photographed for *before* and *after,*
nothing active is in it to be revealed.

I am made of sand. My friends
confide in me, knowing I have no hands.

Score

Would you still have looked terse
or rigorously bored,

if I had only noticed, as you did,
the branch's loom, the skylight's clean incline

across a teenage attic's scoured boards,
like a collapsing ladder by Franz Kline?

What left me averse
to trying out your number afterwards?

How could you have known
the proleptic electric violin's

chalk honing itself on chalk was par for the course
on a single by Manchester's King of the Slums?

And what to make, now, of a Goth girl's hair,
or the bedevilment of wings

developing on State Street, the great scare
of pigeons lifting off in their loud horde—

our looking up from tree-limb to tree-limb,
as seemingly-permanent, gravity-struck and dumb

as a whole day of Rockland County's dim,
persistent rain's continuing alarms?

A Barren Orange Tree

after Lorca

Summer, and my own malice
at seeing myself leafless,
congeal in me, and size me up
    as if I were their root.
Woodsman, cut my shadow from me,
Cut my shadow off.

I was not born, but grafted,
by gardeners who mastered
economies of pits and twigs,
    each from its proper fruit,

who measured and awarded
attention to the ravaged
along the ruts and lanes where moss
    and pebbles mock each root.
Woodsman, cut my shadow from me,
Cut my shadow off.

I see each dry night, like me,
reduced to its assembly
of individual hard stars—each
    far-off thought my root;

rain hangs on me and scours
my conscience in its mirrors,
stiff lockets which evaporate
    and are my only fruit.
Woodsman, cut my shadow from me,
Cut my shadow off.

When time has made me senseless
of time and my dimensions,
I will have great dreams; I will dream
    that fire-ants are my fruit,

and that the chalky menace
my knots and galls embellish,
proliferative, cancerous, shows
    my restoring root.
Woodsman, cut my shadow from me;
Cut my shadow off.

Aftermath

From bed, I counted shiny parking meters,
their single-file chorus by the fence—
your palace guard, or else discovered traitors,
each armored head pinned up on his own lance.

Tiresias

squinting, comes to me in a pair of half-rusted
faces on a coin, or as both sides

of one coin. When he wakes, without breasts
and horrified, the gods

can pummel him with questions: where
is fancy bred? Since you're a man
again, which sex

do you prefer? He won't
answer, but their ex-
cruciating thunder can divine

what he would have: exposed, his outward parts
curl up, a rosy snail
that wants to be a rose.

He's voted the wrong side.
His thighs will be the last thing he will see.

• • •

Blinded, he learned the delicate arts

of teaching heroes to expect disasters,
but saved one truth for preadolescents, old men,

spinsters, and unmarriageable bastards—
a truth which might be engraved in this odd coin's

insides, between the obverse, a scowling patron,
and the flip side, where a sky-blue patch obscures

either a beardless pikeman with an eyesore
or a distraught girl lifting a carnation.

After the Death of Jaime Gil de Biedma

after Jaime Gil de Biedma

Across the patio or in the garden, reading,
the house's shadow obscures
the page; the penitent cold, the end of August,
turns my thoughts backwards, to you.

This garden and its house approach
the birdsong in the complicated trees;
the absence of August, when it grows dark, gets lost,
and your book falls from my hand like the end of the year

in which you died. If only, in that winter
of your last sights, you had been given a glimpse
of sweetness, a taste of light! But I don't

think so. What I want to remember now
are not the hours, the last year,
of your beating your head against cabinets, drunken months, bruises
you collected, old coins, lining your body
like a too-tight clown suit . . . the others come back,
the year before and the year before and the years
before those years, and wash away
the only time we couldn't photograph.

It's your garden. It's August. Wine in vases,
tipsy incursions into your swimming pool,
soft heat under the trees. Voices bring
names: Angél, Juan, Marcelino, Maria
Rosa, Joaquina—Joaquina first of all,
the girl with the whispery, almost-invisible breasts.

The telephone laughed and you came back outdoors
and more of us, you said, would be on their way.
I remember, then, your one-yard run,
the flash of your body exploding into the water.

And nights of total liberty
in your enormous house: everything was for us,
as if we had occupied an abandoned convent,
destroying nostalgias, pulling up secret doors,
sprinting here and there through the open bedrooms
prying open the closets, alternately
amusing ourselves standing naked and fancily dressed,
dusting off, for ourselves
to wear, short gowns,
high boots and slacks, making arbitrary scenes,
the old erotic dreams of your adolescence,
or of everyone's, of a boy left by himself.

Remember Carmina,
Carmina who came late, plump, tiptoeing downstairs
showing us her backside, wobbling
because she held up, in her left hand, a lit candelabra?

Then there were the corresponding months
and months of pain, of paralytic mornings,
the last night of pills and vomit over the carpet.
Later I saved myself, at least, by writing
"After the Death of Jaime Gil de Biedma."

Between us, you were clearly the better writer.
Now I should know what the point of it was, your desire
to dream only ironies, of the muffled romances
in your poems I like best—for example, in "Pandemic."
How can I know what my poems would have been without you?

But sometimes I think it was me, in the end, who taught you.
—Who taught you to take over my old dreams
out of my cowardice: who ruined your own.

2

Music, we could say, provides us with an intensely subjective sense of being sociable. . . . [I]dentity comes from the outside, not the inside; it is something we put or try on, not something we reveal or discover.

—Simon Frith, *Performing Rites*

Mods

Pete Townshend of the Who
puts the silver ball in motion
as the rock opera, his 1969 magnum
opus, *prepares to open.*

Kenny Pickett of the Creation
splits the piñata, London,
wide open with his violin
bow. It is a heightened

standard, to which Edward Ball of the Times
will repair, his sore thumb
cocked for a ride home
from the cellar of crayons, tabby cats, mimes

and cardboard boxes where Daniel
Treacy's semi-annual
dream of a gas that will cleanse the world
of adults comes true. It's splendid,

but Paul Weller of the Jam
contemplates King William
I's life story: the United Kingdom,
he thinks, reveres him, but can't understand him.

"Oblivious" b/w "Orchid Girl"

Green red lantern-yellow and cold-coal
blue, the photo-repro-process dots
are portals, or portholes,
through which the wind of southern Scotland weaves;
his turned-up cowboy collar curves
into a crown of hills, of feathery hills
around which a loose pebble of ash
might roll. His cigarette's

furred, orange
tip's smoke spins out across the picture plane.
The name of the boy is Roddy Frame,
of Aztec Camera, aged eighteen. He hides
his eyes from listeners inside a fan
of flour-ish hair; when the A-side is played
his bangs revolve above him, like an ang-

el's. Think of him as the not-yet-beaten
prince over the water; then these tunes,
half-cribbed from "Eight Miles High," are spies' pigeons
circling south to him, hooks tied to signs
about his plan for taking back his nation—

For the reedy tone
in which he tells their tremulous private things,
for the charm-bracelet chimes from his secondhand pink
12-string,

he will be brought to London, given a band
and half a lifetime contract, and soon owned.

He will outgrow his cold associations.
So that the last I hear of him

before his exile, his synthesized recantations,
is this: "Oblivious" with "Orchid Girl,"
the little-known B-side that ends in exhortation
to an ingenue: "Don't spend
your money. Orchid girl, you make"—or "made"—
"my day." Along the inner groove
a slow parade of proper nouns
goes round after the 45
is done: dates, copyrights. *Postcard. Rough Trade.*

Rereading Science Fiction

So hot nothing stands up except the teasel
Working its will out in the college yard;
Each head swings to announce its independence,
Salutes departing porters with its leaves.

Seen from indoors, the bracts are Fabergés
As shown on dodgy black-and-white TVs;
Are microphone-caps, buckyfullerenes,

Or, better, the beehive-tops of the slender future
Towers, all chromium and curvature,
Atop the clean Manhattan all far-sighted,
Nearsighted white American *Astounding
Stories*–reading teens knew would arrive
By the year 2000 in 1965.
Slim bridges reinforced against strong breezes,
Monorails skim and change along the buds.

Or else they're capsules from that world, stuck here
In inappropriate green miniature;
Once stranded, quickly burying thin roots . . .

One inch high, and hidden in a sepal,
Would you look up and overhear a crew
Talk through the takeoff—escape velocity,

How long before 186,000
Miles per second, and how far to go?
Or else: —*I wonder where this Earth went wrong,*

How it diverged from ours . . .
                        Wind picks them up
So that the bracts bob gently, meaning "no."
The upturned leaves create pools after rain
To drown bugs in for protein.
                        Look: bindweed
Slinks over the nest of leaves at the base of a stem;
Wound-up like DNA, keeping its secret
Tug and drag, the vine deploys,
Each inch or so, a white mute low-slung badge.

Next year, a solid alabaster hedge.

Astronomy

This morning's snapshot-takers in the Bodleian's
courtyard shunt one another from sightlines—
its tanned, gym-toned right angles shrug them off.   .
Inside, we know nowhere less bodily—
night-sky-blue volumes wink from higher floors.

No one needs, now, to start from scratch grown-up
or play connect-the-dots to make a language;
yet our oldest tradition's to claim we've had no tradition,
like swearing to bring no notes to exams—
what could be more American, or duller,

than to repudiate oneself nonstop,
painstakingly self-cultivated flower
forever still-unfolding in its steeple?
Summer-school students tessellate these quads
all afternoon; their cross-

legged cliques split grass up into constellations—
the Spectacles, the Ankh, the Open Book.
At that age anything can matter most
and nothing has to—that's what I was told
later . . . was I them, ever? At fourteen,

my bruiseproof denim-jacket armor painted
with dancing turtles on a field of stars,
I was unselfbelittling enough
for taciturn camp counselors to love—
trailing the older boys' off-campus quests,

clambering back indoors at five past curfew
having found no one; when the staff looked up
from playing Hearts to answer the alarm
and let me go by, I was their small star,
being what they thanked God they had outgrown.

The Epistolarians

for Emily Walker

In British summer time our lucky stars,
      if we can call them ours,
show up for us five hours a night or less;
we come out before they do, and the gulls
stay up like boys on E and never tire,
and will not be translated from thin air.
      They circle Clonmacnoise.

Hitchhiking here took hours. Here the Shannon,
      almost to the horizon,
threw out its long arms far enough to keep
reclusive scholars, salmon, geese and perch
to salt and trade for cloth and metal ploughs.
Here ruins are. Here once the tides enticed
      new friars from their sleep

to hang up nets at sunrise, and stand up
      preoccupied by script,
in candlesmoke made bearable by breeze,
in drafty chambers where their Latin rang . . .
The monks were ours; they were a schooltime spent
preserving something for its gravity
      we torture where it is,

and tell ourselves to savor once it ends.
      Flint slants where the salt winds
strike anywhere, and slap back any wing,
and kiss or taunt and take the rim-worn stones
apart to smooth and never give them back—
stalwarts that hold each other's weight and lean
      on nothing else, and spring

old floorplans on new travellers. Their creed
      turns lintels to its code;
their corbels stand, unpromising, unfair,
preserved for studying, until they fail . . .
Our lives are what we learn, or learn to steal.
Because where more than two of us can see
      or hear each other, there

can be no private place for the sublime;
      since we would not be tombs
of useless wonder; as we are afraid
of shrinking into experts on ourselves,
      we correspond, and need

      such secret languages
as kings abandoned and we made our own.

To the Southern Hemisphere

James K. Baxter, New Zealand poet,
Catholic and commune leader, 1926–1972

What would a thought make of itself, what would thought
Make of itself if it were honest, what

Would a thought, drawn out, given time, make itself
Out to be?—some fishing-rod stick-insect,

Chitinous legs, hooked feelers, a dream of wind,
Some predatory scrap a swallow's catch

Might well ignore. The *Daily Telegraph*
Is full of physics lately: how the sun

Will turn out bad like over-leavened dough,
Puff out and fall back, blackened, and leave behind

Carbonized solids for whatever is left

Of the animal kingdom to eat and breathe,
How it will happen sooner than we thought.

"News that stays news," as the young spearhead said.

But you stay news, too, James—Hemi—New Zealand
Louse-gatherer, ditch-digger, wanna-be

St. Francis, dialectician, latrine-celebrator,
Tutua—nobody—you called yourself, not without reason,

In Maori, not in English, not without reason.

My country's flag stands slowly on the moon
Like a boy in a raincoat-hood at a bus-stop,

Like a Cartesian I. I used to think

That Byrd and Peary, the ice-bearded
Grimacers on my picture books, had seen

The North and South Poles for real, stuck like pearl pins
Through clear tape into a blinding white balloon,

Like that child's magic trick: why doesn't it break?
Your son who at thirteen gave up his Buddhist

Rote you admired, and chose needle drugs

To puncture the same thoughts: why is it your poems
Don't tell us, among the women they

Praise, which was his mother? *Ou tis,* te tutua,

Rainy-day half-saint, there are things you hid
I want to discover myself and will never discover;

You make me afraid. Here most of the way up
The Northern Hemisphere's bell curve, where light rain

Skips from the Isle of Man to the Isle of Dogs,
For a predictable minute its one-eyed drops

Obscure the storefronts and the bus to London
Costs £5.50 return with a student fare

And you stare us down like the highest card in a hand,
And I am the Jack of Diamonds, winking back

At a loss and wet hair hangs down in front of my eyes

Like the scraggly plants at the top of a cave:
Nobody has blinded me and stolen from me!

From under tide-mud, from under the unemployed
Huts, tents and houses you shared with the unemployed

In Hiruharama, if I have that right,
Over the sea your whole life overlooks,

You come and blind us in our only eye

And make us like you, love you. To reach you
My thought is a diameter, a stick-pin

Gone clear to the other side of the world and beyond,
To the flag we forgot to take back, on the only

Face of the moon we can see, standing still in no light

That anyone, maybe, will ever go back to,
Like a tent-pole. You whipped yourself red and white

With the end of a belt, you gave the balance of
Your food away, because it didn't

Count. My country's flag is the one on the moon,
Like a tent-pole,

Like a fishing rod left behind by itself in thin sand,
Where the fisherman scrambled and clambered free from harm.

Blenheim Revisited

for Adam Schwartzman

> . . . *I addressed a butterfly on a pea-blossom thus:*
> *'Beautiful Psyche, soul of a blossom, that art visiting*
> *and hovering over thy former friends whom thou hast*
> *left!' Had I forgot the caterpillar? Or did I dream like*
> *a mad metaphysician that the caterpillar's hunger for*
> *plants was self-love, recollection, and a lust that in its*
> *next state resolved itself into love?*
> —S. T. Coleridge, *Anima Poetae*

Glassed-in, grid-shadowed, camouflaged, held tight
In rudiments of twigs, or almost lost
Like riggings in the roof's slant-salted light—
Evasive, age- and weightless as Descartes'
First axiom, a fleet of x-and-y's,
Heraldic absolutes, the butterflies
Were their own net.
                So many being there,
It cheapened them, as if to lose a few
Were just to lose examples of a type
Which could survive no matter what we did.
So thin, such heated and elaborate
Defensiveness, their motions might announce
Their own fragility as if a boast
Or caution aimed at us, to our surprise,
Who wandered in the banyans taking notes:

Some perched on water in their plastic cup;
Others held clear wings folded—bubble-wrap,
Or the Wright Brothers' model come to rest,

A flight museum's prize behind cracked glass.
Open like matchbooks, sorted like team badges,
A few aspired, reversed, from wire bridges
To just miss a warm draft or catch a mate.
On fruit cut and set out for them, some crawled
Among the seeds like seeds, in their firm coats'
Exaggerated drab, ten shades of brown
And as if crawling were their only motion—
Unnecessary, necessary, prone,
Concealed position of the newly-saved
And -visited all summer. Under shade,
The world they made was mathematical,
Each point's imaginary counterpart,
Alive and in the wild, outside the house,
Distinguished by an *i,*
                              which doesn't count . . .

This is the month, and this the only season,
When after strenuous renunciations
We see ourselves as traitors to a nation
Of scholars paralyzed by observation:

The stars and planets keep their constant motion,
The air survives its winds, the sun its stations,
The waters ebb and flow to their completion,
No doubt to teach us that the end of reason
Is this: that we should ever be in action.

After that hothouse and its long description
The foyer's backlit exits and directions
Led us to outdoor summer air, its chill
Like a suspended sentence, over moss
Concurrent on the walks like circuitry.
The Perspex doors behind us linked, then locked:
Bells closed the day. Cars started from their lots.

From reading in the plane back, I learned how
Lungfish who learned to breathe by hiding out
Under their beaches grew to love low tides,
Then tadpoles, then reptiles, mammals, us;
From satisfaction, sea, unconsciousness,
They grew without a goal. Soon, over Queens,
The evening baseball diamonds stared back up
Enviously at us. Overdue
Manhattan wheeled and needled into view;
Then roaring, and the nightlight, innervated,
Prodigious runway set to meet us as
We rose above ourselves, then hit the ground.

The Wind from the 1950s

Randall Jarrell's daughters are still riding
Behind him in an open-topped sports car

Of 1957, streamlined, plush
And spotlessly maintained. They look back from it

With hair too short to be blown back by the wind,
They look back as if clinging to the spine

And haunch of the leopard that sprints in the National Zoo,
Whose enlightened hosts have built for it

A cage like a savannah in a cage.
They're really his stepdaughters. From the nest

The driver's seat makes for him, from his split-
At-both-ends beard and tipped-back shades, he grins,
His rose cheeks taut. He looks at home among them.

• • •

Election Night: Rock Creek sorts colored stones,
Turns mill wheels, joins a never-used canal

(Steam trains took all its traffic from day one).
Counting close races on the radio,

I thought of justice, one of the mud-choked paths,
Developing, returning to no source;
Of silver crowns coins thrown in water raise;

Of Katharine Hepburn on the roof in *Desk Set,*
Skyscraper-top wind cooling her bag lunch.

She's a reference librarian scared of losing her job
To the megacomputer whose hierophant and guide

Is Spencer Tracy, who can't tie his shoes.
He staggers with the luggage of the breeze

Beating about his coat, dragging him down,
Then lifts his sandwich from his lips and asks

(Reads from his clipboard) *When you meet someone
For the first time, what's the first thing you notice?*

His checklist's flapping: *Eyes. Hair. Accent. Gait.*
Reaction shot. Amused. Red hair, green eyes:
Whether that person is (pauses) *a man, or a woman.*

Unseasonal

A summer morning in winter,
                    meat in the air.
Packets, dispensed, of aerosol rain.
The college town's cathedral square

is like a children's refuge; grownup stars

have tried hard to see out.

Since Mardi Gras is soon, the stone
guys standing up in doorways wear fake jewels.

Corroded—what?—white oak leaves have survived;

as black as photograms, as thin as prints,
they are blown from the roof slowly, their own means.

            An unaccompanied piano—

            "Just because I walked in on you singing
            in the bathroom, doesn't mean you were bad! You
                            were good!"

Each kind of person persons claim to be,
or claim to have been, turns into a place

we treat as means to reach

any of them, before they go away.

Ocean State

for Forrest Gander & C. D. Wright

If the car has stalled by the mall in the shape of a star
it must be for a reason
                  look around: courage
the sea is in sight
                  it has no name

Your water tower hangs in exclamation
swelling
                  over Warwick, R.I.
holding its shape as if never giving out
holding   as if giving nothing away
too slick for a roost
                  its claim *Come and choose wrong*

                  what distinguishes what humans built
from what is human   it stands unmoved in rain

Ford Escorts mill outside the glass arcade
Accords   hold to obstreperous queues
sad puppy   what are you waiting for

old quarries hope
                  shapeless as diaries
unform'd   ovariform   or multiform

the gradualism of water has left them their salt

ramage   ransack   leave no thing behind

3

Beth Ellen looked at Janie as though her last hope had washed out to sea. In fact it had, because Harriet was relentless. "Beth Ellen, listen to this. If I don't see your parents, how am I going to know what they're like? Answer me that. How am I going to know?"

—Louise Fitzhugh, *The Long Secret*

Christic in the House of Martha and Mary, by Velázquez

Because her home is someone else's castle,
She stands in our end of the picture, braced
Against her wet wood table and brass pestle
    Where shadows splash diffuse
Stormclouds across the bone-dry masonry.
Dismembered cloves of garlic that refuse
    To grind themselves to paste

Tally before her like a daisy-clock
The hours she has stood for, supervised
    By an arthritic, pocked,
Sad woman mentioned nowhere in the Gospels—
The hours which four perch, slim silver bells,
    Have spent shinily pending
Dismemberment to feed a house of five

And God Himself spent lecturing to Mary.
Seen only through a drafty, shade-chilled square
    Hole cut into a wall,
Christ, Lazarus and Mary rest, secure
Sun, Mars and Venus of an orrery,
Resplendent in their sense of an unending,
    Simple and categorical

Exemption from all earthly labor, granted,
	However, only to the first
Dozen or so who have the luck to take
Advantage of His offer. For the rest—
	Skeptics, the housebound, day-to-day
Providers, younger sisters and the like—
The kitchen table and a sullen duty.

	—So Martha thinks,
Looks bitterly to us in ruddy silence
Only because she has no one to thank.
	She wants to be rescued;
Her full lips pursed, she looks about to cry
And won't do. We're her only audience,
Or else Velázquez is, who, not yet twenty,

	Abandoned his Seville's
Provincial tutors and unleavened houses
To strut his brushwork for the court and King,
	And brought Madrid this canvas
Recording the albedo of two eggs,
The weft of hair, the gamut of fish scales,
And the half-stifled hopes of all the young

Who, while the bright elect practice, converse
	And hope to be immortal,
Grind garlic, skin the fish and set the table;
	Who, were the tables turned,
Might say their faith in art or faith or manners
Counts more than the dull skills they never learned,
Then sit down calmly and expect their dinner.

David with the Head of Goliath, by Donatello

Mud threaded into hair
Behind him, lips too wide,
Goliath's blackened eyes lose all their focus as we stare:
He floats away on his expansive beard
In which the boy hero of Israel seems to wade.
　　　　His spotless sword
Picks at the beaten temples as at weeds
That cling to swimmers' ankles at high tide.

One hand against his firm
And concave hip—a swan's
Head balancing his stone below the swan's-neck of the arm,
The swan's-wing of his undeveloped chest—
He might be looking for his father's farm;
　　　　His airy stance
Proclaims *Of all things beauty is the best;*
Second is self-sufficiency, the charm

To which all strong things yield,
And not to have grown up a distant third.
Below, slack-tethered goats patrol the trampled battlefield;
Uriah might be watching from the plain,
Shielding his eyes, and if without regard
　　　　For glory of his own,
Expecting peace, glad of it, and prepared
For home, for his new wife, for their small yard.

Bareheaded, still too young
To give commands, Saul's son
Looks uphill, rapt, into the hard, articulated shrine
Of thighs and shoulders and their new allure;
Sunburnt outside their tents, the soldiers sing,
David has slain
His tens of thousands, as if they were sure
Which one of them would live to be a king.

St. Cecilia at a Reed Organ,
by Orazio Gentileschi and Giovanni Lanfranco

for Sara Marcus

Her tutelary angel has arrived
And isn't needed; touches down, and bends
To hold a page of music for the saint,
Whose instrument—
Red keyboard, wooden housing, metal tent—
    At rest, arrests,
In its fine net of touches, both her hands.

Her wrists and half-unrolled, unruly sleeves
Are hovering; a ringlet by one ear
Fades into blonder air;
The unembarrassed rubrics of her blush
Defend her concentration like a wish,
    Distract us, and protect
A tutor trying not to understand

That nothing can be taught her anymore.
That look, attentive and remembering,
And wait-forever posture and shut wings
Describe the cares
Cecilia won't know again; she hears
    Before her the whole score,
And rises to its memorized demands.

"What We Are All Missing," by Man Ray

A meerschaum pipe, laid almost horizontal
on the fulcrum of its scale,

supports, in its old bowl, a durable bubble
of rigorously-blown glass, whose green-and-purple

ripple
embellishes a niece's fingernail.

Posterity

Randall Jarrell, Greensboro, NC, Nov. 25, 1963

Eaves shift the wind indoors.
He's watched the funeral broadcast all day:
The proud men in whose hands we put the world
Have cast themselves as shadows, and recede. The streaky, coy,
    Obliterating snow
The static makes reminds him of his beard's,
And is as past repair. A year ago

    In Washington, D.C.,
The Cuban missile crisis having cancelled
His sherry on the South Lawn –the known world
Up for renewal, like exhausted television shows –
    He had consoled
Himself describing color folios
Of astronomical photography:

*   All the dim future stars*
The galaxies give birth to, each untouched,
Translucent bubble parent to some world,
And all this in one shrinking patch of space—if something ends,
*   How infinitely much*
There is that isn't ending! Up the stairs,
An open window rattles where its blinds

Contain the roar
A power mower raises from a lawn;
In the far mower-operator's world
Nothing has changed. Burnt oniongrass and oil char the air.
Fifty next year,
Not old enough to take defeat as fun,
Jarrell picks up his pipe and locks his door,

Eyes level with the stem
Long use and ash have cured of its aplomb:
Tonight he means to finish *The Lost World.*
Mildew and onionskin—his boyhood letters, disinterred
From rural Hollywood—
Wait in the kitchen: stacked, assembled words,
Addressed to calm adults, who understood.

4

"I should almost like to go for a long walk in the dark with you," said Jane. "Yet I want to get to the party. I know what there's going to be: ice-cream. *Yet I keep thinking once the party starts we're getting nearer to the end of it. Then what shall we have to look forward to?"*

—Rosamond Lehmann, *The Gipsy's Baby*

Over Nevada

One aileron corrects itself, oblique,
Abstracting air. It lifts it, then unbends.

Of the hard road and the omnipresence of winter,
Of hardy silence, cabin, spike and stake,
Others can tell you more.
                              O find a lens,
Redaction of all telescopes, to show you
All dwellings and all persons far below you,
And how could you stand to go anywhere?
                              It is the splinter,
Privilege, call it, that keeps you alert or awake
As the fissure and suture of mountains unrolls and the lake
And decades of inequitable snow,
Like graphs of the casino owners' take.
How could you ever sort out or pay back what you owe
In that white coin, language, which melts as you start to speak?

Inventory

for Simone Bakst

Our last summer-school students have gone home
to what's left of their summers, and what's left
is only landscape: the unlined black grass
a one-to-one-scale star map pinned with rain.

Our attic classrooms, locked, bright outside, bear
on their Doric supporters: unused chalk!
White regiment of silences! raised hands
never called on! Cold marble! porcelain mugs!

Rows of globe lights outside the shut school-theater
are the zeros in one million. A million and one.

But yesterday evening, inside, a babble of Hamlets;
a Rosalind; murderous mountain boys;
taciturn brides, gymnastic, smart kid sisters—

If my whole life
could be played out again, played more like yours!
Ghosts of departed quantities, you were
more real than what you copied down all day,
all summer; we cannot go back

to adequate devotions, rapid-fire
emoluments of names, half-empty boards
whose black scoured flatness no spotlight can pierce.
Rhetoric sucks! If I did anyone good
he or she was like me: nothing else.
Discarded drafts, stripped paperbacks, high shelves:
nothing I said can have taught you how to act.

For the last time, our highway back downtown
lies lit up like a ladder on its side,
one tall enough to use to hang a scrim
or fly a girl in harness from gas tanks
and powerlines, and land her on her feet.
How can we hear you now? What can we know
of you and not ourselves?
                                    Fit audience,
match-colored headlights scrutinize the dark.

On the *Patriot*

Right angles. From the train, they are a slew
of vacancies, poles pinned above the flats
where dirty ice declines to onionskin,
each shrinking 1 in upright isolation,

except that they recoil from our motion,
seeming to lean backwards, as if they knew
that we were rattling towards them with our grids,
we for whom things connect. Power shuts down,

then kicks back in: New Haven passes, then
Old Saybrook, then a string of gravestone-gray
lakes strung together by chain links of ice,
now breaking up below a bank of reeds
from which the mainland shrinks. What this country needs
is a good

            I fell asleep
before the state line, and now I forget
what I had meant to follow—five good
senses? A five-finger exercise,
a bracing five-star twilight, or five lines

spent on this suddenly swaying iron horse
I'm in, which, true to decade, doesn't smoke?
Five smoky kinds of gray, or six at most,
are all you'd need for this Rhode Island coast

we're passing now: matte, uninflected sky,
pale scratched-in clouds, a pencil-lead horizon,
squalls turning ocean brighter and uneven,

an opal shoreline, and a broad last stripe
for the foreshortened beach's stretch of linen,
a washed-out banner waiting for its slogan.

—A slogan, say, about this sight
and silence, and the grid between them, how
they stand for us, or will.
                    Deaf President Now
might do: the "barricades" of Gallaudet,

a thousand students rushing to propel
their tides of placards down North Capitol.
The college field grew its own wood,
green phalanxes of protesters in tents;

reporters settled in like orioles
back from the winter, nesting under goal-
posts, under satellites. A crowd

lay down in driveways to prevent
the wrong president's presence. Their own hands
were winning. They would not be spoken for.

Kingston, R.I., is next. Maples arrive
in line beside our tracks, and wave. Snow scars
and slows the branches down like second thoughts:

what makes a nation? Can a boy salute
two flags at once? Treetops shrug off their queues
of shiny wires, startled; the train stalls;

bright, brittle, and sequestered, new leaves pull
themselves upright, point out, and fingerspell
their answers—deaf to which, each thick trunk stands

beside itself, uneasy with the use
I've made of it, its cluster of thin hands
conversing with the glass, checking for ours.

The Alders

after Jaime Gil de Biedma: Ribera de los Alisos

*which by corrupt or accustomed speaking they com-
monly call the Elder . . . doth serve . . . to lay the
foundations of buildings upon, which are laid in the
rivers, fens, or other standing waters, because it never
rotteth in the water, but lasteth as it were forever.*
(OED)

The banks are much too old.
                    The path goes down,
dirty from sand and full of scratches, bruised
like all the scratches I wore as a boy;
abraded rootlets stick out here and there.
Telescoped, down the river, the knotted poplars
seal everything off—are all I can want from the world,
from this world, as its gestures show me back
into the first few seasons of my life.

A tiny corner of the map of Spain
is what I know of memory, was my one kingdom;
fixed, sheltered, here, I imagine myself there,
no time has passed—
I am six, that age
at which one goes to bed certain to sleep,
and wakes, with eyes defiantly still closed,
laid out along the bed on winter mornings,
and imagines a favorite day, the previous spring,
suffused by plain and calming odors,

pines? But these things change—are hard to notice;
abscond into leafmeal, or into the path itself,
the path I have been undoing by walking it.
Such sleeps, such grade-school dreams, are indices,
and all I remember of them are images:
one night a horse, one night the birth,
terribly impure and difficult, of the moon,
or the high flashes of a river approaching,
carrying under it many years, floods in September,
the exaltation and fear of being alone
when I was walking late to school and knew it—

before these thoughts, there are no others;
I would know what I was if I knew what I could have
                                        called them.
And I know there is nothing we see that does not mix up
beauty and truth; still,
the beautiful hieroglyphs, images poured from a story,
are not the whole story—

there were, too, so many months of October,
of coming home after dark singing, when the wind
of autumn put its knife blade to my lips,
and of excitement in the family room
twinned with the fire, when nothing was unfamiliar:
the rhythm of the house and of wooden train stations,
the sweetness of an artificial order,
rustic and thinly spread, like a mat of peat,
a life like one of the woodsmen or grenadiers
who stood, steamed flat forever, on my wallpaper.

How can I simply stand above it now
or simply resent what I must have wanted then?
But how can I not see there the books of accounts,
the comical ghosts of school-fees, no slight wind
or specialized valley has yet been able to calm?

                  The farther boughs
like brushes play their snare drums in the wind,
and something else gets ready to grow dark,
as jumbled as these alder needles, as far
below me now as the vertiginous stream—
a softening, profound affinity
for nature where there is none, for company
wherever I think there might be none to be found,
and a fear of what is, before which these points and blades,
each pointing its unsheathed way to the one far creek,
seem far from me again; I am far from myself,
and the sash of the water, the banks with their needles,
                            their alders,
are flimsy, antique, too sad to disregard.

Letter from Minorca

after Jaime Gil de Biedma

After the distant nightclubs and their piers
had cut off lamps for curfew, quiet laws
descended on our island
and on our neighbors inland;
a fingernail, a residue of light
rose up before dawn on the facing beach—

a thoughtful phosphorescence, a thin gaze,
a parachute afloat. So near that sea,
from the planning-mistake of the wooden boulevard,
where we waited for hours for the townies' night
to shut down for us, there seemed to fly toward us,

again and again, the sense of being enormous,
part of the atmosphere, clarified, so that the docks,
their rush and scrappy nettles, took up space
nowhere, or just *inside* the two of us . . .

Next day was your last there. All the flat sand
gathered and lapsed in bodies of its own,
bodies that lay on one shoulder each, and could cry,
for love, all day in stiff clouds without tears.
If you kissed them they tasted of oysters and nectarines;
from far away, they smelled like liberty.
When you fell asleep outdoors, late and alone, nostalgia
grew like a bloom over envy and desire,
nostalgia for what you must have considered another
age of the body, of unrefined desire—

Not desire alone; also the sense
that someone desired you too. It is this dream,
the same monotonous dream throughout adolescence,
the same old dream, of course, and more remote
each time it happens. Shame, erosion, prudence—
wrecking and excavating old foundations
to put up new resorts—collect from love,
as from old dune-walls, all the stones it has,
dismantling it for wisdom or for money . . .

Tomorrow, no moon in the daytime; no sea; the City,
pink angled marble, beams, a kind of beauty;
standees on trains, a kind of library.
The night after tomorrow you will sit up,
still sleeping, and remember the sand on the bodies'
El Dorado, the given,
the gold, the choosy, the brazen
untainted because unattained, the ones you will never
know if you could have known; and the imprecise grace
of knowing *that,* at least, will get to you
like a slap in the face; you will swivel, smart, and see
nobody has touched you—what do you owe, anyway,
and to whom?—and wake up half-erect
already, and have forgotten even that debt.

Connecticut Toccata

1

Things are trying to be other things.

The air above the Green's rigid with ash
as if the crisp, illegal
private burning of leaves
continued, today, all across New England,
but it's just
one danger, in one place
the fire engines' tritones try to find—
they cut the bulky traffic as our God
sliced us a path once through the Sea of Reeds.

                          Two days to Halloween—
the square-jawed, irredeem-
ably square Minuteman,
eyes level with the light at York and Main,
boast cherry lips; he's changed, or come undone,
or out. He's blowing kisses at our Mall
from his afloral pedestal
and going nowhere—patriotic dream
or princess swivelhips,
he's changed it all and still can't get away.

68

2

Where faint, metallic, periodic lights
strop the two-lane road east to Providence
between the coastal towns,
where mist peels fishtins over valley lots
schoolbuses pack for night and weekend stays,

tonight the billboard spots, the Merit stations,
the rural road half lit like tracing paper,
the hour's delay, are a life repudiated.
Fields blank as dial tones on New Year's Eve
are one-way broadcasts of fertility,
broad coupled consonants spilled in clean rows.
Whitman lies in New Jersey, spacious rant
of continental foliage now dried
to sober coastlines whose dreadnoughts are dregs.
What grows up for him now? Where auto-parts
and what were once called malt shops and are still
galleries where the local mating arts
are tried and tested, shine in emptiness
and cleanliness, and next to that, bright light,

shoreline light, flat light, Alexandra, you
used five years up here, and left when you could;
learned here to make Coke-cans and pipes from scraps;
love, now, a Holland of chess-clubs, tea-towels,
where no one can be late for an appointment,
and the plain church surmounts a Mondrian-
plain city center, inland, ironed, dried.

Snack bars look closed,
and the still-visible, the last few stars,
straining, by now barely hold one another apart.

3

Lights dangle from above the ice rink's door,
its steely ribs swell high and gather leaves—
its pregame dusk
is water as the home fans file in,
the water of
the hardly visible lamplighter fish
that mulls the gravel on its trench's floor
and eats whatever's close enough to see—
brine shrimp, silt, wire, soaked cloth, sea-parsley, glass.

Cheers rise inside. It's hot. They're making stars.
An ambulance stares, open, at glass doors.
Ice jams the small cracks in the third-floor window,
replacing glass itself, as streets replaced
footpaths, the footpaths grass, the grass old seas,
new grass old roads, and over the new grass,
new monuments posed for
half-frozen chiselers,
with the resolve we know from Milton's daughters—
who fell to bed to work when he woke up
so not one word was lost—

or the resolve of the Lady of Christ's himself,
proud, celibate, at Cambridge,
ransacking books to make he knew not what
for who knows whom, whose tutors made him start
his enterprise by arguing in Latin
That Nature is Not Subject to Old Age.

Home

Stuck freeway sprawl from Milford to New Haven,
then blinding spackle off Long Island Sound.
On a Subaru hatchback packed as if to elope,
a tangle of bungee cords and patched-up rope
keeps down
the I-frame of a sky-blue bicycle.

Its rear wheel spins; the riverine, uneven
spokes tilt, shuffle and scramble figure and ground:

a girl's reward for moving; a cymbal; a gamble;
a sketch out of *Ringworld*; a heliotrope;
a hypnotism test. A magnet-school
physics-club's show of centripetal
force. A gestalt-psychologist's working model
of an episcotister, or tachistoscope.

Shipbuilding Towns in Connecticut
and Rhode Island

The second time they looked soberer, thickening, stiff
Shut houses and girded skeletons, less enthralled
With their own diminishments, like a career
Now stalled. From the stalled train, the Hubbell Memorial
Technical Center, with its illegible slogan,
And its redshifted paint have this in common:
They "want to be wanted," not as children want,
For whom a second chance at rewards too far
Past next week is hard to imagine, but as an aunt

Might by a new boyfriend or blouse flaunt at Thanksgiving
Having settled for something else, as one kind of divorce
Casts life as an awful game show: will you have
This less-than-what-you-hoped-for oven, or what
That curtain-sized calendar hides? And this explains
Why it is so American to split up,
Since we are told from grade school on to trust
The future, not the present—still less to assume
That what's gone before, with its limits, will come again.
The other family members can take their own chances,

Like Bridgeport, for example, or like these
Sousaphone smokestacks nobody annotates now,
Or you do, thinking mostly about cousins
Who might have been made of snow, so dimly alive
They were then, laden with job security
Or confidence in the fruitfulness of their labors,
Their immigrant's sense of the law, and the latch unpicked

Through which we might have been desperate not to see
Ourselves with no faces, as spearcarriers or contrarian
Thersites types, or countertenors and basses.
Whoever the lucky lead turns out to be
We don't know. Don't ask us. It's not who you think it is.
Yellow and blunt and peeled and haptic red,
Individualized, coming off the trees,
The prodigies declare themselves as such,

And fall down all over one another. The prodigals
Come back just after that, and build their mansions
On top of or beside the compost of their older
Brothers and sisters, the never-entirely-decayed,
Never-attended school-leavers who accomplished
The tasks they were taught to perform, the ones whose merit
Remains open to question, but they were at least
Labor-intensive, deliberate, ready and pure
And starchy, and if ever to be of use
To the ones who would come afterwards and make
Something of themselves, had to be thoroughly done
And done first, if they were to be done at all.

Essay on Mass Transit Subsidies

When this journalist crossed the country by bus, what he met
Were people who had been crossing the country by bus:
I want to confront the person who has been
Declaring me dead, and find out why,
One said. That was some way of putting it! Maybe the best,
Or the hardest to answer. Once we have glorified all
The small towns, what will the next set of kids be left
To aspire to get away from? You wanted to have
Been one of the constellations I saw this morning,
Not in the vault which will still, next year, be being cleaned,
But in the pitch-dark through which the trains return,
And now we think we should celebrate home by leaving
Some sign of having despised it behind. Always some
Chariot seems to us to have been double parked,
Floridian low-lights a sad pink, left on all night,
A reason to be glad we had never bothered—
Being angiosperms to their mosses—to learn to drive,
And have to trust the conductor with her sense
That the goals are always practical, that no one
Would want to stay on all the way. Now only five stops
Separate us from our longed-for afternoon meal.

Road Movie with Food

My atlas is soaked. And another
Thing: most sound effects in movies
Are not made on set, but in Waterford, Connecticut,
On lots, where most of the work in the world gets done.
Staid, excited back-

Seat driver, hopeful deluge
Or delusion, arriving with umbrellas
Secured under each arm, I miss you a lot:
I miss your wiles, your democratic hat
With roses up the blue side, and your faith

That people neither you nor I see have
Interior motives, that they, too, can taste
Salt in new greens, and savor the rest we crave.
Was it for this the young cooks hoped, when catkins
Hearkened to heels and currents, and gusts that branded

Dissolute meadows, and water voles
And curious, pink, endangered species of bats,
Though minor, loomed large in one another's concern?
The new lament factories all smell like braised meat.
Sleek and intestate, without a will of its own,

The stale chain of in-house rewards they might win now extends
Its braided links past Norman, Oklahoma,
Into Normal, Illinois, almost crossing
These United States from stem to stern,
Top to bottom, and back to front, once and for all.

Arriving Clouds

To notice dispassionately the blotchy, squared-
Off glass frontier of the International School
Across the walk is to know
Their world was too large: its allies keeping
Still, the ginger children who have fled
Out over railings, through each recessed door,
Will come back soon: I'd like to call them ours,

If they haven't been claimed. Then a white
Lynx crossed my path. Tolerance and
Withdrawal are valid models (she said) of all things,
From space travel to nutmeg and to love:
You get what you want, need more, and with extraordinary
Timing and cuisine they need you back.
Their names are Princess, Vitamin and Reliable.
They run up great phone bills. To tell

The truth, I'm practically next to Texas
Here: the scarp of the south tip,
Its large flat handle, and then the uneven slides
That wouldn't touch given all day. It comes with peppers,
Raucous, auricular, rice- or sugar-
Filled, and small: around them we bake dust
In frosty shapes cut out to look like doves
Or hamburgers, or like the conversations
Scattered all over this road in Mystic, Connecticut,
That taste good nevertheless, and are bad for you.

First Mornings in New York

for Claudia Gonson

Thick sprigs of holly paint-stained by mistake
stick by their tack-ends to the iron fence
squat painters and card-salesmen stood beside,
whose chained-up gear banged on the rails all night,
accordions as tuneless as an index.
The music drags, the street musicians stay;

canebrakes of leather and discarded boys,
too willing to be discarded to look discarded,
still span the sidewalk catwalks at St Mark's—
I'm happier to see them there, some days,
than to see friends . . . unstuck, precipitous,
hearing myself, I blush and then admit

my sour wish to elegize the living.
Youth isn't wasted, it outlives the young;
the steely Argo will survive its parts
and reach its port with every nail renewed,
its job to cross water, corrode and be renewed.
Each morning the Williamsburg Bridge commuters look out,

brake, turn, dodge, spit and swerve past the onramps;
only cabdrivers' passengers look back
to watch Delancey Street greet the unseen—
four-story high billboards of optimist
commercial painters rampant, bearing cans,
cartoon speech-bubbles poised above the cars:

Welcome to Manhattan. Compare and Save.

A Sudden Rain in the Green Mountains

for Jessica Bennett

Plush hills, the raw materials, fall away.
The soaking clay
In which the serried oaks, the picturesque
And swaybacked pines, elected to evolve,
The famous marble in its bare reserve,

Vanish like guesses in these verticals
Whose heft at dusk
Blurs roofs to ridges, veils the bicycles
And splashes where they lean hard into curves.
Looming like crowds, such weather makes its world;

Its crash and draft and spate and uniform
Consonant force confirm
Or mean—not that without you there are no
Attainments I can care for or call good—
But that among them, missing you, I know
How much delight, green need

And weird vivacious luck drew me to you:
Luck lasts with us. Out here I can believe
That all companionships only rehearse
Or faintly copy ours, and make it plain—
As over the plain inn, the plain roof clears—
That granite, marble, nascent evening stars
And that impressive dinner bell, the moon,

Still seem—may seem, to me, forever—yours,
A portraitist's surround to set you off
For admiration and comparison.
In light you spare, unevenly, they shine
To give such thought, your thought, occasion,
Triangulate, and show me where you are.
I'm not with you. I will be with you soon.

Altar to the Egyptian Goddess Bast

Marie is my cat. Her eyes are compared, like seas,
like days. She will abandon visitors,
examine them, climb windows to follow them home.
We had to grow out of it. Have you shared the feeling
that your groceries were keeping a secret, or were a lie?

Marie hunts supervillains. Her stripes berate.
When she sleeps lengthwise her ribs scroll, tackle and glow.
Marie doesn't know where Arcadia or Australia
or asymptotes used to be. She grew up there.
For *Australia* read *Rockville*. For *Rockville* read *name of home*.

Marie is a star and she works the clouds by night;
she is not a planet and should not be interfered with.
In the animal hospital yesterday she took my name;
they offered her spools, rolled thread. She followed them.
Marie has been spayed. She smiled, their work to see.

This is a test for you from my Marie.
Points will be taken off for answers in which
she finds no examples. This could go on for years,
like the stock market, or for exactly the time
it takes to grow up, grow breasts, grow in wisdom, grow rings.

Marie would like to thank you and lick your lips.
I haven't discovered my style but I'm still trying.
Today rash gulls will argue away the walls
to get to their foods. Marie will not stop them on time.
Marie is also known as Ariel,

girl-tamer of horses, unmercifully teased—
who had the best erasers in the class,
who fled to Montana and cherished the science fiction
she stowed in her hat, in her fingernails, inside her purse.
She might curl up under you, under your twills, for a treat.

Twice nightly her brackish monuments wag their tails,
meaning *naughty, precocious*. They smile. Their work is to grow.
Marie is explicit, treads water. She wants to see.

NOTES AND CREDITS

"Sheep in Fog" ("**Persephone [Unplugged]**") is a poem by Sylvia Plath; a "Les Paul" is a long-admired model of electric guitar, made by the Gibson company, and named for the pre-rock pop singer who helped perfect the instrument.

The italicized lines in "**Day-Lilies at Night**" quote *As You Like It;* the phrase "fear success" I take from Carol Gilligan's *In a Different Voice.* • Elizabeth Smart (1913–86) wrote *By Grand Central Station I Sat Down and Wept* and *The Assumption of the Rogues and Rascals.* • Herzliyya is an affluent seaside suburb of Tel Aviv.

Lines 1–4 of "**Mods**" appeared (as prose, and verbatim) in the *New York Times,* March 28, 1993, in an article on the Broadway version of *Tommy.* Readers of "Mods" may want to know that Daniel Treacy's band (1978–present) is called the Television Personalities; that Edward Ball, whose own band is called the Times, was an original member of the TVPs; and that they covered songs by the Creation (1967–69). William the Conqueror, of course, spoke Norman French. • " '**Oblivious' b/w 'Orchid Girl'** " is a wonderful 1983 single by Roddy Frame's band, Aztec Camera, released in the U.K. on the record label Rough Trade. The first single by Aztec Camera came out in 1981 on the independent Glasgow-based label Postcard Records, whose slogan (impressed on all its releases) was "The Sound of Young Scotland." 45 rpm was once the normal playing speed of a seven-inch vinyl single;

"The Forty-Five" was the Jacobite uprising of 1745, the last serious military challenge from Scotland to Hanoverian rule. • **"Rereading Science Fiction"** was inspired partly by Scott McCloud's comic book *ZOT!,* partly by Andy Roberts and Jenni Scott. • Clonmacnoise (**"The Epistolarians"**) lies south of Athlone, on the Shannon; during the Middle Ages it harbored a powerful Irish monastic community. "E" is a British colloquial name for the drug Ecstasy. The word "epistolarian" owes its currency to Tim Alborn. • In **"To the Southern Hemisphere,"** the line "Poetry is news that stays news" is an aphorism of Ezra Pound's. "Hemi" is "James" in Maori phonemes and was the name Baxter used in his commune. "Tutua" means "nobody" in Maori (and also "slave"); Baxter calls himself "te tutua," "the nobody," in one of his sonnets. *Ou tis* means "nothing" or "nobody" in ancient Greek, and is the "name" Odysseus gave out as his own to the Cyclops. "Hiruharama"— "Jerusalem" phonetically in Maori—was the name of Baxter's commune. • Italics in **"Blenheim Revisited"** adapt sentences from Robert Burton's *Anatomy of Melancholy.* • Italics in **"The Wind from the 1950s"** quote the movie *Desk Set.* • Italics in **"Ocean State"** quote Philip Larkin; the "water tower's" original can be found in C. D. Wright's poem "Like Peaches."

Italics in **"Posterity"** quote, slightly altered, a letter of Randall Jarrell's to Adrienne Rich, in *The Letters of Randall Jarrell.* One line in "Posterity" and one line in "The Epistolarians" adapt phrases of R. P. Blackmur's.

"Ghosts of departed quantities" (from **"Inventory"**) was Bishop Berkeley's dismissive description of calculus; Jordan Ellenberg brought the phrase to my attention. • The *Patriot* (**"On the *Patriot*"**) is one of the Amtrak trains on the Northeast Corridor (Washington-to-Boston) route; the poem also alludes to events at Gallaudet College in Washington, D.C., whose deaf students protested the trustees' selection of a hearing president. She soon resigned, and the trustees appointed Gallaudet's first deaf president, Dr. I. King Jordan. "What this country needs is a good five-cent cigar" was once a current phrase, attributed to Thomas R. Marshall. • In **"Connecticut Toccata,"** "the Lady" was the nickname Milton received from his schoolmates at Christ's College, Cambridge. "That Nature is Not Subject to Old Age" is Merritt Hughes's English translation of "Natura non pati senium," one of Milton's early Latin poems, probably written for and at Cambridge. • The italics in **"Essay on Mass Transit Subsidies"** quote a Greyhound bus rider in a *Washington Post Magazine* feature story from the mid-1990s. • Two lines in **"Altar to the Egyptian Goddess Bast"** started life in a letter from Alice May Williams to Mount Wilson Observatory; Drew Daniel showed me the letter.